MIGUEL CABRERA

Awesome Athletes

Jameson Anderson

Checkerboard Library

An Imprint of Abdo Publishing
www.abdopublishing.com

www.abdopublishing.com

Published by Abdo Publishing, a division of ABDO, PO Box 398166, Minneapolis, Minnesota 55439. Copyright © 2015 by Abdo Consulting Group, Inc. International copyrights reserved in all countries. No part of this book may be reproduced in any form without written permission from the publisher. Checkerboard Library™ is a trademark and logo of Abdo Publishing.

Printed in the United States of America, North Mankato, Minnesota.
052014
092014

THIS BOOK CONTAINS
RECYCLED MATERIALS
Cover Photo: AP Images
Interior Photos: AP Images pp. 7, 9, 13, 19; Corbis pp. 23, 25, 29; Getty Images pp. 1, 5, 11, 15, 17, 20, 21, 22, 26, 27

Series Coordinator: Tamara L. Britton
Editors: Tamara L. Britton, Megan M. Gunderson
Art Direction: Neil Klinepier

Library of Congress Cataloging-in-Publication Data

Anderson, Jameson.
  Miguel Cabrera / Jameson Anderson.
     pages cm. -- (Awesome athletes)
  Includes index.
  ISBN 978-1-62403-328-5
1. Cabrera, Miguel, 1983---Juvenile literature. 2. Baseball players--Venezuela--Biography--Juvenile literature. I. Title.
  GV865.C25A64 2015
  796.357092--dc23
  [B]
                          2013048643

TABLE OF CONTENTS

THE TRIPLE CROWN

On October 3, 2012, Miguel Cabrera was about to become a baseball legend. It was the last game of the season, a night game in Kansas City, Missouri. Cabrera was in position to win the American League (AL) **Triple Crown**.

But Cabrera's home run lead was slim. He led Texas Rangers outfielder Josh Hamilton by just one run. Cabrera had 44 home runs. Hamilton had 43. If Hamilton hit a home run that night, the two would end the season with a tie. Cabrera would lose the Crown.

In the Tigers **dugout**, players watched the Rangers game on laptop computers. But Hamilton did not homer in the Rangers' 12–5 loss to the Oakland A's. Cabrera was the 2012 AL Triple Crown winner!

Cabrera finished the season with 44 home runs, 139 runs batted in (RBIs), and a .330 **batting average**. But Cabrera was less excited about his award than that the Tigers had made the **playoffs**. Would they make it to the **World Series**?

FUN FACT BEFORE CABRERA, THE LAST TRIPLE CROWN WAS WON BY BOSTON RED SOX SLUGGER CARL YASTRZEMSKI IN 1967.

HIGHLIGHT REEL

José Miguel Cabrera was born in Maracay, Venezuela.
1983

Cabrera married Rosangel Polanco.
2001

The Marlins traded Cabrera to the Detroit Tigers.
2007

The Detroit Tigers made it to the postseason but lost to the Boston Red Sox in the ALCS.
2013

1999
Sixteen-year-old Cabrera signed a contract with the Florida Marlins worth $1.8 million.

2003
Cabrera was promoted to the major leagues; the Florida Marlins defeated the New York Yankees four games to two in the World Series.

2012
The San Francisco Giants swept the Detroit Tigers to win the World Series; Cabrera won the American League Triple Crown.

6

MIGUEL CABRERA

DOB: April 18, 1983
Ht: 6'4"
Wt: 240
Position: 1B
Number: 24
Bats: Right
Throws: Right

CAREER STATISTICS:

Batting Avg:	.321
HR:	365
RBIs:	1260

AWARDS:

All-Star: 2004–2007; 2010–2013
MVP: 2012, 2013
Silver Slugger: 2005, 2006, 2010, 2012, 2013
Triple Crown: 2012
World Series: 2003 (Win), 2012

ALL IN THE FAMILY

José Miguel Cabrera was born in Maracay, Venezuela, on April 18, 1983. His parents called him Miguel. Miguel's family lived in the La Parera neighborhood. Their small house had a kitchen, a bathroom, and two other rooms.

From an early age, Miguel's life was filled with baseball. His father, also named Miguel, played baseball on several Venezuelan teams. Miguel's mother, Gregoria, spent 14 years playing **shortstop** for the Venezuelan national softball team.

Miguel's family lived next to Maracay Stadium. Miguel watched his father and his uncle play baseball there. Miguel and his younger sister, Ruth, quickly learned the game. Miguel and Ruth sometimes practiced together. They used a stick for a bat and wadded up a piece of paper for a ball.

Today, young players still attend baseball school at Maracay Stadium.

UNCERTAIN FUTURE

As much as Miguel loved the game, his father did not want him to play professional baseball. His father thought Miguel should be an engineer. An engineer would have a better chance of raising a family in a nicer neighborhood.

To that end, Miguel's father expected Miguel to pay attention in school and get good grades. He wanted Miguel to go to college. Miguel promised his father he would focus on his schoolwork. When Miguel wasn't studying, he liked to play basketball and volleyball. But baseball was always his favorite.

Miguel spent a lot of time practicing with his uncle David Torres. When Torres was a young man, he was drafted by the St. Louis Cardinals. He played in the **minor leagues**. Torres helped Miguel develop his baseball skills.

Fellow Maracay resident Dave Concepción was another of Miguel's mentors. Concepción spent 18 years at shortstop with the Cincinnati Reds and won two World Series with the Big Red Machine.

Baseball, Basketball, Hockey, Football

The Sporting News

Price: 75 Cents

APRIL 26, 1975

A RARE TALENT
David Concepcion
Cincinnati Reds

PHOTO BY MALCOLM EMMONS

A DREAM COME TRUE

When Miguel was 14 years old, he told his father that he wanted to play **Major League Baseball**. Miguel's father agreed. But he said Miguel had to keep getting good grades in school.

Miguel continued to play baseball. He worked to improve his skills. **Scouts** from teams such as the Minnesota Twins, New York Yankees, and Los Angeles Dodgers traveled to Venezuela to watch Miguel. They wanted to see if he was ready to play in the **minor leagues**.

However, baseball rules say that a player cannot sign a contract until he is 16 years old. So, the scouts kept an eye on Miguel. They knew he would be a star when he was older.

In 1999, Miguel turned 16 years old. He stood 6 feet 2 inches (2 m 5 cm) tall and weighed 185 pounds (84 kg). Several teams wanted to sign him. Each offered more money than the last. Finally, Miguel and his family chose the Florida Marlins.

Sixteen-year-old Miguel's first contract paid him $1.8 million.

MINOR MIRACLE

During his first year in the **minor leagues**, Cabrera played **shortstop** for the Rookie-level Gulf Coast League Marlins. His **batting average** was .260, he had 22 RBIs, and his 57 hits included 2 home runs. He finished the season in Class A Short Season. There, Cabrera averaged .250 and brought in 6 runners for the New York Penn League Utica Blue Sox.

In 2001 after 57 games, Cabrera was promoted to Class A. He played for the Kane County Cougars of the Midwest League. There, in 422 trips to the plate, he got 113 hits. Seven of them were home runs! Cabrera scored 61 runs and batted in another 66.

Cabrera did so well in Class A that **Major League Baseball** officials selected him to play in the Futures Game during **All-Star Game** weekend. Cabrera played on the World All-Stars team, which lost to the US All-Stars team 5–1.

MINOR LEAGUE BASEBALL

MiLB IS DIVIDED INTO SIX CLASSES

Triple-A
Double-A
Class A Advanced
Class A
Class A Short Season
Rookie

Players begin in the Rookie class and advance as their play improves.

Cabrera batted .268 for the Kane County Cougars.

FUTURES GAME

THE FUTURES GAME IS PART OF ALL-STAR WEEKEND. IN THE GAME, A TEAM OF PROSPECTS FROM THE UNITED STATES PLAYS AGAINST A TEAM OF RISING STARS FROM ELSEWHERE IN THE WORLD. CABRERA WAS THE YOUNGEST PLAYER IN THE 2001 FUTURES GAME.

THE MAJORS

On June 17, 2001, Cabrera married Rosangel Polanco. The couple had known each other since they were teenagers. The Cabreras would go on to have three children, daughters Rosangel and Isabella, and son Christopher.

When the 2002 season began, Cabrera played third base for the Class A Advanced Jupiter Hammerheads of the Florida State League. There, Cabrera's **batting average** was .274 and his 134 hits included 9 homers. He earned a second trip to the Futures Game. This time, Cabrera's World All-Stars defeated the US All-Stars 5–1.

In 2003, Cabrera was promoted to Double-A. He was batting .365 with 10 home runs and 59 RBIs for the Carolina League Carolina Mudcats when he was called up to the majors. At just 20 years old, Cabrera became a member of the Florida Marlins.

A 20-year-old Cabrera poses in his Marlins uniform.

WORLD SERIES WINNER

On June 20, 2003, Cabrera was ready for his first game with the Marlins. During his first time under the big league lights, he hit a walk-off home run to win the game!

Cabrera wasn't needed at the **shortstop** position, however. And, Mike Lowell was playing well at third base. So the team had to assign Cabrera to another position. He learned to play left field.

The Marlins' success led to a **playoff** run that year. The Marlins beat the San Francisco Giants in the National League Division Series (NLDS) three games to one.

The Marlins captured the **pennant** with a 4–3 victory over the Chicago Cubs in the National League Championship Series (NLCS). The team advanced to the **World Series**. There, they faced the New York Yankees.

Cabrera connects on a three-run homer in Game 7 of the NLCS.

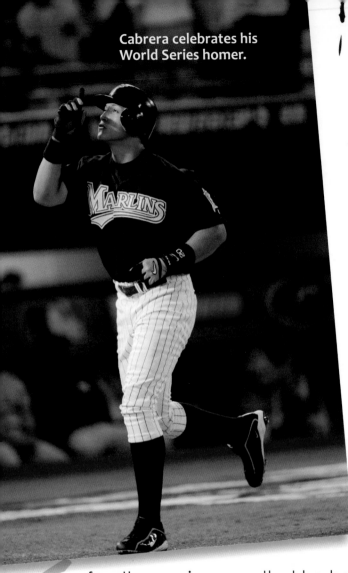

Cabrera celebrates his World Series homer.

Florida grabbed Game 1 of the Series. But the Yankees came back and took the next two games. In Game 4, Cabrera hit a two-run homer off Roger Clemens in the first inning on the way to a Marlins victory. The Yankees would not win another game. The Florida Marlins won the 2003 **World Series** 4–2.

Cabrera had much more success with the Marlins. During the 2007 season, he drove in 119 RBIs. It was the fourth year in a row that he had brought home more than 100 base runners. Cabrera also averaged 31 home runs each of these seasons.

Though Cabrera was doing well with the Marlins, the team went 71–91 for the 2007 season. The team's management needed to make changes. So on December 7, the Marlins traded Cabrera to the Detroit Tigers.

The Marlins' 2003 victory was just the second World Series title in team history.

A NEW BEGINNING

Cabrera was disappointed in being traded. He liked playing for the Marlins. But he decided to make the best of the situation. He arrived in Detroit ready to make a new start.

The Detroit Tigers' owners made sure Cabrera was happy on his new team. They signed him to an eight-year, $152.3 million contract. At the time, it was the fourth largest contract in the history of baseball.

Detroit fans were quick to embrace their new first baseman, whom they nicknamed Miggy.

In his first game as a Tiger, Cabrera homered in the fifth inning of a 5–4 Tigers loss to the Kansas City Royals.

Early in the 2008 season, Tigers manager Jim Leyland decided to move Cabrera to first base. Cabrera had played first base some in the **minor leagues**. He quickly adjusted to his new position.

AN OFF SEASON

In 2009, Cabrera made the news for a bad reason. He drank too much alcohol one night. He got into trouble with the police.

Yet Cabrera was still a professional on the field. That year, his **batting average** was .324 with 198 hits and 34 home runs. He scored more runs than any other Tiger.

The Tigers finished the season 86–76, the exact same record as the Minnesota Twins. According to baseball rules, the two teams had to have a **playoff** game. The winner would go on to face the New York Yankees in the **postseason**.

The Twins beat the Tigers 6–5. The Tigers missed out on a chance to make the playoffs. Some fans blamed Cabrera. They said that his off-field behavior had distracted the team.

Cabrera scored in the third inning, but it wasn't enough to stop the Twins.

BACK ON TOP

The Tigers went 81–81 in 2010 and again missed the **playoffs**. The following year, the Tigers met the Texas Rangers in the American League Championship Series (ALCS) but lost 4–2.

Before the 2012 season, the Tigers signed first baseman Prince Fielder from the Milwaukee Brewers. Cabrera was glad to have another power hitter on the team. He moved to third base so Fielder could play first base.

The two were a threat to opposing pitchers. That year, Cabrera won the American League **Triple Crown** and was voted Most Valuable Player(MVP).

Cabrera and Fielder gave Detroit a powerful one-two punch, but the Tigers traded Fielder to the Texas Rangers in 2013.

In the **playoffs**, the Tigers beat the Oakland A's and went on to sweep the New York Yankees. For the second time in his career, Cabrera was heading to the **World Series**. But the Tigers lost the Series when the San Francisco Giants swept them 4–0. While the Tigers didn't do well in the World Series, Cabrera had the best year of his career.

Cabrera homered in Game 4 of the 2012 World Series, but in four games, his 13 trips to the plate resulted in only three hits.

PLAYING IT FORWARD

In 2013, Cabrera averaged .348, hit 44 home runs, and was again voted league MVP. The Tigers faced the Boston Red Sox in the ALCS. Detroit won the first game, but the Sox came back to win the next two. Detroit won again in Game 4. After that it was all Boston. The Sox beat the Tigers 4–2.

In the off-season, the Tigers wanted to make sure Cabrera stayed with the team. So on March 14, 2014, Cabrera signed a contract extension worth $292 million over ten years. It was the largest contract in American professional sports history.

When Cabrera isn't playing baseball, he spends time with his wife and their children. His family lives in Florida and also spends time in Venezuela.

Cabrera also focuses on making the world better for children who don't have good baseball fields in their

Cabrera plays catch with his son Christopher at the 2013 All-Star Game.

neighborhoods. In 2012, he started the Miguel Cabrera Foundation. This group raises money to help improve and build baseball parks in the United States and Venezuela.

Cabrera wants other children to have the experience that he has had with baseball. He knows that all over the world there are children who love to play the game. He hopes to help those children achieve their dreams of playing **Major League Baseball**.

GLOSSARY

All-Star Game - a game between the American League All-Stars and the National League All-Stars.

batting average - the number of hits a batter gets divided by the number of the batter's at-bats.

dugout - the seating area for team members who are not currently on the playing field.

Major League Baseball - the highest level of professional baseball. It is made up of the American League and the National League. It is also called the majors.

Minor League Baseball - the five classes of professional baseball that are lower level than the major leagues. It is also called the minors.

pennant - the award won by the champions of the American League and the National League.

playoffs - a series of games that determine which team will win a championship.

postseason - the time immediately following the regular season when teams play each other to determine which teams are in the playoffs.

scout - a person who evaluates the talent of amateur athletes to determine if they would have success in the pros.

shortstop - a player who defends the area between second and third base.

Triple Crown - an award given to a player who leads the league in home runs, runs batted in, and batting average at the end of the regular season.

World Series - the annual championship between the American League champions and the National League champions.

To learn more about Awesome Athletes, visit **booklinks.abdopublishing.com**. These links are routinely monitored and updated to provide the most current information available.

INDEX